INFORMATION EXPLORER JUNIOR

Record It!
Shooting and Editing Digital Video

by Shauna Masura

CHERRY LAKE PUBLISHING · ANN ARBOR, MICHIGAN

A NOTE TO PARENTS AND TEACHERS:
Please remind your children how to stay safe online before they do the activities in this book.

A NOTE TO KIDS:
Always remember your safety comes first!

Published in the United States of America
by Cherry Lake Publishing
Ann Arbor, Michigan
www.cherrylakepublishing.com

Content Adviser: Gail Dickinson, PhD, Associate Professor, Old Dominion University, Norfolk, Virginia

Photo Credits: Cover, ©Pavel Losevsky/Dreamstime.com; page 4, ©iStockphoto.com/ Claudiad; page 6, ©iStockphoto.com/monkeybusinessimages; page 10, ©iStockphoto. com/Ju-Lee; page 11, ©iStockphoto.com/nycshooter; page 12, ©domturner/ Shutterstock, Inc.; page 13, ©Rick Becker-leckrone/Dreamstime.com; page 15, ©Konstantin Sutyagin/Dreamstime.com; page 16, ©iStockphoto.com/baranozdemir; page 17, ©iStockphoto.com/bonniej; page 19, ©iStockphoto.com/CEFutcher; page 22, ©Arvind Balaraman/Shutterstock, Inc.

Library of Congress Cataloging-in-Publication Data
Masura, Shauna.
  Record it! : shooting and editing digital video / by Shauna Masura.
    p. cm. — (Information explorer junior)
  Includes bibliographical references and index.
  Audience: For K to grade 3.
  ISBN 978-1-61080-484-4 (lib. bdg.) — ISBN 978-1-61080-571-1 (e-book) — ISBN 978-1-61080-658-9 (pbk.)
1. Digital cinematography—Juvenile literature. 2. Digital video—Juvenile literature. I. Title.
  TR860.M28 2013
  777—dc23   2012009453

Cherry Lake Publishing would like to acknowledge the work of The Partnership for 21st Century Skills. Please visit www.21stcenturyskills.org for more information.

Printed in the United States of America
Corporate Graphics Inc.
July 2012
CLFA11

Table of Contents

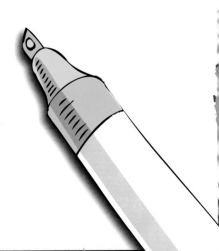

4 CHAPTER ONE
Plan Your Movie

10 CHAPTER TWO
Shoot Your Movie

15 CHAPTER THREE
Edit Your Movie

19 CHAPTER FOUR
Share Your Movie

22 Glossary
23 Find Out More
24 Index
24 About the Author

CHAPTER ONE

Plan Your Movie

Do you like watching movies? Movies are fun to watch. They can entertain us with stories, but they can also teach us a lot about people, places, or events. If you have

What kind of movies do you like to watch?

Use a notebook to keep track of any ideas you have for new movies.

ever wanted to share an event with a lot of people, a movie is a great way to do that! You can make movies for school or for fun. Let's get ready to shoot your own movie.

The first thing you need to do is decide what your movie will be about. Make a list of ideas. Your movie could tell a story from your life or from someone else's life. It could also be a story you made up. Once you

If you're planning a movie for your family to watch, think about what kind of movie they would enjoy most.

choose a topic from your list, you can start planning out your movie. What will happen in the beginning, middle, and end of your movie? While you plan, think about your audience. Who will watch your movie? Classmates? Teachers? Family members? You will want to plan your movie so that it appeals to the people who will be watching it.

Next, you might want to write a **script** for your movie. A script tells the actors every word they will say and provides a plan for what will happen in the story. This is very helpful if you already know how you want your movie to go. But you don't have to use a script if you don't want to. Another idea is to have the actors make up the words while they are filming the movie.

Movie Script by William

A script will help you plan out your ideas before you begin shooting.

Storyboards are a great way to organize your shots.

Last, you must plan your **shots**. You can do this by creating a **storyboard**. Think about how each part of your movie will look, feel, and sound. Different shots and angles have different effects and can give your movie a cool look. Long shots show a person's whole body. Close-up shots only show the face and shoulders. Try to film from different angles: from the front, from the side, or from above. Each new shot can change the way you show your ideas.

To get a copy of this activity, visit www.cherrylakepublishing.com/activities.

Activity

Imagine your class is learning about healthy food. You can make a movie to show your classmates how to make a healthy snack. First, create a storyboard to help you plan your movie. A storyboard is a series of boxes that show each **scene** in a story. Draw a picture in each box to show what your scene will look like. Then write a short sentence underneath.

CHAPTER TWO

Shoot Your Movie

You need a camera to shoot your movie. There are different kinds of cameras. Many of them only take still pictures. You will need

You can't start shooting your movie until you have a camera.

Most modern cell phones can record short video clips.

one that shoots video. You may already have one in your home. Many cell phones and computers have built-in video cameras.

Before you film, check to make sure your camera has enough light to show a clear picture. If the room you film in is too dark, your movie might be hard to see. Try to add more light to a room, or go outside to film if it is too dark inside.

Make sure that you film in a quiet place. If there are loud sounds or too many noises in the background, it will be hard to hear your actors. Attaching a **microphone**

A good microphone will make the actors' voices much easier to understand.

Reshoot any parts of your video that don't go right the first time.

to your camera can help your movie sound better.

If your shot does not go the way you wanted it to, you can always shoot it again. When you are all done shooting, ask a grown-up to help you transfer it on a computer.

To get a copy of this activity, visit www.cherrylakepublishing.com/activities.

Activity

Borrow a camera from an adult and try to shoot your healthy snack movie. You and a friend can take turns acting out the scenes from your storyboard and filming the shots. Pay close attention to the light and sound. Don't be afraid to shoot a scene again if you need to.

Make sure each shot turns out just right.

CHAPTER THREE

Edit Your Movie

You've finished filming and loaded your **footage** onto a computer. But you are not done yet! You can use a video editing program such as iMovie or Windows Live

Most new computers come with video editing software.

You can even edit your movie on a tablet computer, if you have the right apps.

Movie Maker on your computer to change parts of your movie. Editing can take a few minutes or it can take a long time. It depends on what you want to add or take away.

You can use the video editing program to cut out scenes that you don't want in your movie. These are called outtakes. Maybe your actor forgot her lines. Maybe the camera was shaky during one scene. You can cut out these parts so they don't show up in the final movie.

You can also add a title in the beginning and credits at the end, just like a movie or a TV show. Some editing programs let you add cool effects or background music.

Once you have cut your outtakes and added effects, save your movie on your computer. Now you are done!

Add some effects and music to put the finishing touches on your movie.

To get a copy of this activity, visit www.cherrylakepublishing.com/activities.

Activity

Film a short movie tour of a room in your house. Put the movie on your computer. Try adding all the effects you can, and then make a new version with only a few effects. See which version of the movie you like better!

Try a variety of different effects.

CHAPTER FOUR

Share Your Movie

Now that you are done, you can share your movie with others. Think of all the ways you can watch a movie. You can play a DVD on your TV, go to a movie theater, or stream a

One way to show your movie is to gather people around your computer screen.

video online. The easiest way to watch your movie is to play it on your computer. You can hold your own viewing with family and friends right in your home.

Do you want to share your movie with classmates or family members who are far away? You can turn your movie into a DVD or put it on a flash drive to watch on another computer. You can also ask a grown-up to

Burn your movie to a DVD if you want to watch it on your TV.

To get a copy of this activity, visit www.cherrylakepublishing.com/activities.

Activity

Have an adult e-mail your movie to people you know. Ask them to send an e-mail back to you with their ideas or comments. This will help you improve your skills when you make your next movie!

E-mail is a great way to send your movie to people.

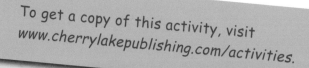

upload it online. An adult can e-mail it to people you know or post it on a Web site for others to see.

Shooting a movie is a fun way to share ideas. Anyone can do it if he or she knows how to plan, shoot, edit, and share. Ready to get started? Lights! Camera! Action!

Glossary

footage (FUT-ij) recorded video

microphone (MYE-kruh-fone) a device used to record sound
or make sound louder

scene (SEEN) a part of a movie that shows what is happening
in one particular place and time

script (SKRIPT) the written text of a movie

shots (SHAHTS) individual pieces of footage that are edited
together to create scenes

storyboard (STOR-ee-bord) a visual plan of the shots a movie
will include

Find Out More

BOOK

Grabham, Tim. *Movie Maker*. Somerville, MA: Candlewick Press,
    2010.

WEB SITE

PBS Kids—Arthur: Movie Maker

http://pbskids.org/arthur/games/moviemaker/moviemaker.html

Learn more about making movies with this fun game.

Index

actors, 7, 12, 14, 16
angles, 8
audience, 6, 20, 21

cameras, 10–11, 13,
   14, 17
cell phones, 11
close-up shots, 8
computers, 11, 13,
   15, 16, 17, 18, 20
credits, 17

DVDs, 19, 20

editing, 15–17
effects, 8, 17, 18
e-mail, 21

flash drives, 20

ideas, 5, 8, 21
iMovie, 15

light, 11–12, 14
lines, 16
long shots, 8

microphones, 12–13
music, 17

outtakes, 16–17

planning, 5–8, 9

scenes, 9, 14, 16–17

script, 7
sharing, 5, 19-21
shots, 8, 13, 14
sound, 8, 12–13, 14
storyboards, 8, 9,
   14
streaming, 19–20,
   20–21

theaters, 19
titles, 17
topics, 5–6

Web sites, 21
Windows Live
   Movie Maker,
   15–16

About the Author

Shauna Masura is a graduate student from Rolling Meadows, Illinois, studying Library and Information Science at the University of Michigan.